Finding Simba

LETTY NEAL

NEAL PUBLISHING

Copyright © 2025 by Letty Neal

Finding Simba: written 2015

All rights reserved.

ISBN print: 978-1-922492-52-4

No part of this publication may be reproduced, distributed, or transmitted in any form or by any means, including photocopying, recording, or other electronic or mechanical methods, without the prior written permission of the publisher.

For permission requests, contact sallylindaharris@gmail.com

For privacy reasons, some names, locations, and dates may have been changed.

Book Cover by Inki Publishing

Finding Simba

Background

My parents did not have a lot of money when I was born. They lived in a little house on the edge of the slums in Peterborough and I remember the smells of the numerous drains, the cinder lanes, the dingy dwellings, the absence of flowers and the ragged people with their love of fun and laughter.

However, Mother gave me great gifts. She fostered my imagination by her stories and by beautiful books she bought me.

She had my blond hair cut at *Slaughters* and then she pressed in the waves. She bought my well cut winter coat from London. At seven years I was sent to ballet classes. Also I was sent to a little private Froebel school similar to Montessori. I blossomed. I passed the exam to grammar school.

Chapter One

FIRST LOVE IS WONDERFUL

I have only been attracted to about five men in my life. They were all brave, adventurous, strong men and most of them had well-made bodies. They were practical and survivors. They knew how to look after their loved ones in times of danger but could be difficult in everyday life. They were very basic in their manner but knew how to put on the old charm when they wanted something or someone. I married the first one; the others I just looked at and hardly touched. One of them, younger than me by twelve years, has just died at sixty-nine. What a waste of a still great character – handsome, fit and adventurous.

In 1945 I was fifteen years old and very innocent

when I met Norman, called Tub. He had a baby face and was seventeen. My mother was giving me a big party in the Conservative rooms on 1st January 1946 and I needed to ask more boys, so Pearl Wright, who wore make up at school and knew lots of boys, said she would help. She suggested I ask Tub because she liked him as a friend.

Norman at 17.

The next day when I was delivering Tub's invitation through his letter box, I was in my old-fashioned riding trousers that did nothing for my figure. I quickly rode off on my bike while Tub's father, Jimmy Neal, looked at my rounded bottom curving out from my tiny waist and, knowing my name was really Miss Broadhead, christened me Miss Broadbottom.

I found later that Tub had seen me earlier when I had visited Big Hall at his King's School (founded by Henry the Eighth). He was peering down from the upstairs landing, which was the old minstrel's gallery, when he saw me and decided he would like me as a girl friend. I was dressed in my GTC uniform because I was a Girls Training Cadet preparing for the forces (a very much milder form of Hitler's Youth). I remember I was wearing a tight navy skirt and a startling white blouse beautifully washed and ironed by mother, and I was very proud of my one red stripe, for good service, sewn on the top of my sleeve.

Me at 17 looking very serious in the GTC.

After receiving the party invitation, Tub soon rang me up and said we ought to get to know each other if he was coming to my party. We arranged a dance at the Town Hall and he would collect me. By now our family was living in quite a large house in a posh part of Eastfield Road, Peterborough. Good girls were always called for. Tub was only the second boyfriend to call for me at my house. The first one was Peter Boizot who I liked as a friend. Later, he was the first person to open fast food pizza restaurants in England and Europe and, when older, was included in a list of one the richest people in England. He never married.

When Norman rang our bell my father Reg rushed to answer and there was Tub resplendent in a suit with his mackintosh carried over one shoulder. Father, having as usual taken off his disposable collar and with his braces dangling, looked him up and down and noticing his sturdy frame said, "You look strong enough to protect her." Father, who was very young at heart, gave a giggle and ushered Norman into the kitchen to meet my family who were all gathered there.

Tub and I were both shy and were both virgins. Although he was really naughty and had a wicked sense of humour, he was very charming and soon had me writing in my diary: *I think Tub is the nicest boy I have ever met*. The party was a great success and when we played passing the parcel Tub won the prize for the most comfortable lap to sit on and I won the prize for the best hair style wearing my blond hair waved over one eye like the film star Veronica Lake. The party ended by everybody forming a long line and dancing the conga down the stairs and along the shopping arcade, which we all thought very daring.

In the next few weeks Norman and I went often to the town hall where he danced with a natural rhythm and held me tightly around the waist. This was a safe area of the body. Only the bad girls let a man's hands stray and if they gave their favours to lots of men they were called 'the village bicycle' and were deemed unsafe to marry. It was quite all right for the men to have passionate affairs; indeed some girls preferred a man with a little bit of experience. When an invitation arrived for us to attend a party at one of his friend's place I managed to erase the name Tub for his proper name, Norman, and from then on always called him Norman.

When I cycled to my Grammar School for young ladies wearing my brief school tunic and long brown serge knickers, I would pass Norman's King's School where he would often be standing by the ancient door wearing his long prefect's gown. I would give him a quick wave while he would give a long gracious one befitting a school prefect.

Half a mile away we both had sports fields that were next door to each other. Here Norman played rugger or was hockey goalkeeper. He wore my school scarf to bring him luck. I was very competitive and ran up the hockey field on legs that had danced ballet for six years. My waist was so tiny that Norman could circle it with his two hands. I was always determined to win and my teacher described my play as, 'Like a bull in a china shop.'

Chapter Two

MEETING THE FAMILY

Me at 8.

Our fathers had nothing in common. My father was a

car dealer in the slums where he sold spare parts. Norman's father had a posh office in the cathedral grounds. He was an insurance manager. Norman's father was also in charge of the Dad's Army, the Home Guard, like Captain Mainwaring on the television. At the beginning of the war they had no guns so they used broom handles to march with. He was a kind man but he could be rather pompous and stern while my father had an endearing personality but was just a little like the 'spiv' in the same program. He was a private with flat feet and he could only march for a little while, but he loved the stirring music and he had a tall upright posture and a friendly grin. Norman's mother worked at the fuel office and was well educated and once she corrected my grammar. She was a fun person.

Norm's father Jimmy, marked by cross in centre like Mr Mainwaring, Reg sitting cross legged on right.

Now Norman was my boyfriend but I never told him about my life in the slums as he often did not understand people who were uneducated. There was also a big class distinction in 1946 and when Norman's parents asked me to tea I was a little worried they would not like me.

Norman's parents were educated and they did not eat in the kitchen like my family did. Tea was served at 5.00pm. We looked on these outings as a great treat as food was still rationed even after the war and everybody made a special effort when they had guests.

I was a little in awe of the family at that time and I

was also very shy. Norman obviously wanted his parents to like me and I tried hard to say and do the right things. We were given Welsh rarebit (cheese on toast) as the main course and I had a huge appetite and really enjoyed it so that when there was nothing left except a little bit on my knife, a little pink tongue popped out and wiped it clean up and down the knife to the horror of all the family.

I was not aware my table manners were wanting but Norman soon told me about it. On 1st January 1946 I made a promise: *My New Year resolution is to not worry, never lose my head and to be nice with good manners.* (I found this entry in my 1946 diary). It reminded me that when I was 3 years old and living in the slums a lady had annoyed me and I had said, 'Take your sixpence and tick it up your arse.'

Norman and I both loved walking and nature and the river. Norman had a large collection of wild flowers he had pressed, while ponies and riding were my passion. I was overjoyed to hear Norman wanted to be a vet as we were both animal lovers. In the holidays he worked for the vets Mr Poles senior and his son Sam Poles. They lived just outside Peterborough in Whittlesey and Norman learnt to ride, in a fashion, their big black horse called Rajah so that they could do their visits on horseback. Sam was an outspoken, untidy, dumpy man with a moustache and a wide rascally grin. Sam and I both competed in gymkhanas. He rode a small pony called Nibby while I, determined to win, rode Kelpie who could turn on a sixpence but spent a lot of time rearing at the start of a race. Old Mr Poles was well groomed and bowler-hatted and we both hunted with the Fitzwilliam hunt. I dressed up in a bowler hat and white stock and wore a black jacket and boots and tried to act like a sophisticated lady. These days I would not hunt.

Norman and I went to the noisy Hunt Balls where, in the last post, hunting horns were blown and we galloped around the floor kicking our legs in the air. I was more energetic than Norman. He bought a badly fitting second hand evening suit and took great pride in the black bow around his neck, tying it himself. He said men who bought ready-made ties were cads. He borrowed his father's dancing shoes, worn by upper class people in those days, and he also borrowed his father's white silk scarf and lost it on the way home. His father could be very stern and he made Norman retrace his steps to find it although it was midnight.

My Aunty Letty made me a simple blue lace evening dress in which even my tiny bust showed up, and my perfume was Chanel No. 5, a present from my mum. Norman delighted in buying me a corsage of flowers to pin on my dress but sometimes this clashed horribly with the colour of the dress I wore. After dancing I loved leaning my bare back against the cool marble of the Town Hall columns and it was here I found my first drink of sherry unpleasant, although I loved a little of my father's whisky in my tea.

Norman started to get tired of galloping about the dance floor. He was ready for more intimate love making and said he would have to go out with one of the naughty girls if I did not join in. I told him to go, but he stayed, and he accepted the 'waist only area'. I was enjoying being in love and I wanted to savour it slowly.

Those first seven months of 1946 were among the happiest times of my life. I loved being a selfish teenager when for a while I could think only of myself.

Chapter Three

GETTING TO KNOW HIM

Falling in love for the first time is wonderful. You enter a world that glows with new feelings: the masculine smell of a partner's old tweed jacket, the touch of a broad hand in your tiny one, the excitement of lips pressing on yours, the eyes gazing at you hopefully with longing and the wonderful words of love pouring out of an innocent partner. Even at seventeen Norman had the charm, the gift of words and the ability to chat up and compliment any female he fancied. Our interests were similar and if they weren't we pretended they were. We talked and laughed together and our world was positive.

My pony, Kelpie, now took second place although I still loved to be in his green field full of clover where in the joy of a spring morning I turned somersaults. I loved his special horsy smell as I groomed him and I still giggled with joy when my friend Jennifer and I rode our ponies Brandy and Kelpie, cantering over Lord Fitzwilliam's beautiful land, where we had been given permission to ride. Life was perfect, and then Norman went to the veterinary college in Camden Town London.

Letty and Norman enjoying a dance.

At first we wrote to each other several times a week. I felt my heart jump with joy when I saw his large untidy scrawl on the envelope. The last summer before entering college, the Neal family who did not have a lot of money (my mother said it was because Norman's parents smoked and Mr Neal gave huge sums of money to the Masons and played golf) had been on a Billy Butlin's holiday. Once at this holiday camp, having first paid your money, everything including the sport's facilities, the dances with a proper band and the daily activities like treasure hunts, was free. Holiday makers were housed in small chalets and the only torment was caused by a huge speaker blaring out, "Wakey! Wakey!" very early in the morning and by various loud-mouthed individuals in red coats trying to organize your day.

It was here Norman's mother found a couple from London who were willing to look after her young son while he was at veterinary college, letting him board at their house. They also had a young daughter. In his letters Norman said he had a long expensive journey travelling from his digs to vet college at Camden Town and he did not like the Sunday afternoons at his lodgings, because everybody gathered around the piano to sing 'Hey Ho Come to the Fair'.

To be near his drinking pals in Camden Town, Norman soon moved to a very disreputable road of large old houses that had been turned into flats. He seemed to have new digs every month. In about 1950 I visited him in one of these terrible spooky flats in Rillington Place. In a house opposite, Christie the murderer had lived from 1938 until 1953 when he was charged with the murder of his wife and later hanged. During this time he had killed seven women putting their bodies in the garden or in a cupboard and his wife was buried under the floor boards. I did not like the atmosphere in this road and was frightened. I was horrified to find out later that when I had visited Rillington Place at least two bodies were already buried in the garden opposite and that Christie had been living only twenty feet away from me.

I also visited another flat where Norman had only a sky-light and could sit on the bed to fry his bacon and to wash up. Eventually he joined a gang of vet students in a large, ancient flat which had a row of small bunks and bedrooms and a large but primitive kitchen. Here Sporty, one of his roommates, put a Woodbine cigarette in his mouth to wake him up in the morning. When red-haired Daphne came to stay with Sporty, Norm let them have his bigger bed.

While Norman was in one of these digs he met a pretty, slim, religious girl from a theological training college nearby. She did not believe in strong drink. When he took her to a vet college dance he wanted to please her so he ordered them both lemonades. Later, Norman's hard drinking pals joined them, lining up the pints of beer for him. The girl was shocked and a beautiful friendship soon ended.

Norman's special friend at college and also during his life was Tom, an ex-service man who had been a prisoner of war in Italy. He loved women and was able to escape three times and join willing Italian women in the hills. Each time he was recaptured and was brought back and the Italians were very understanding. Norman had first met Tom on the first day of college when they were both late for a meeting with the Principal, so they went to the pub instead.

Norman showed Tom a picture of a little undeveloped girl that was me, standing beside my pony Kelpie who had lots of rosettes, prizes we had won at gymkhanas, tied to his bridle. It was soon after this the love letters from Norman suddenly stopped.

Me with my pony Kelpie. I am wearing old-fashioned riding jodhpurs bought second-hand. In the war we had clothing coupons and there were not enough to use for riding clothes.

My main passion was my new feeling for Norman

and everyday when I came downstairs my eyes looked to the wire letter holder fixed to the flap in our door to see if there was the familiar envelope with his large bold writing. Then disappointed, but with my pride intact and with a straight back and a raised chin, I went into the kitchen to smile at my grandmother, Ethel. She always had a bright fire burning in the grate and a large cup of tea. I never let my family know I was upset. It would have been too painful to discuss and only when I was alone in my bed at night did I grieve because my love had been cut away.

Chapter Four

NEW BOYFRIENDS

Norman after a few years at college.

I did not write to Norman and it was several months

before he at last sent me a letter. It was Thursday, 21st of November, 1946 and was the only entry in my diary mentioning Norman for three months. It was a horrid letter and began: *For your better information the last letter I wrote you was...* I did not reply to such rubbish. My feelings had altered. I was very busy with my new show mare, a pretty sixteen hands bay mare with a white blaze, although I still had Kelpie. I was also riding horses for Mr Nutt, a marvellous horseman, and most weekends in the summer my family and his were at shows or gymkhanas.

I had lots of boyfriends I really liked and was enjoying life. There was Tony Harris, a great looking guy and super sportsman who was at Oxford. There was Mick Swallow, who was a real 'heart throb'. We took a country walk but were spied on by one of Norman's friends. Another boyfriend was Ken Poulter. He was trained to artificially inseminate cows. There was Bill Poole, who played the piano and was rather sweet. He later became a Captain in the army after studying at Sandhurst. There was Richard whose family collected antique clocks. He drove a little car I called 'a box on wheels'. Ron, an airman, was also my friend as was a boy I called Cockerel, who drove his father's butchers van.

These boys were usually at the Town Hall dances and some of them would take me home. I do not think I kissed any of them but perhaps I did, as I faintly remember one of the boys kissed me and his nose hit mine and it made me giggle. My diary reads: *I had millions of partners.* I have always had an affinity with people who are different.

At sixteen I did not bother with the facts of life, although I had a credit in Biology O levels. I remember when Margaret Stanley asked me to spell 'cuff' backwards, I did so without understanding the meaning which made all the girls in my class roll about with laughter. I lived in my own little world. I liked all the girls in my class and had lots of friends.

Me, renewing my makeup after a swim on the Isle of Jersey.

I was very athletic and had danced ballet for six years. On the Isle of Jersey our family stayed at the Hotel Metropole where there was a band every evening and here I taught my father, Reg, to dance and I had lots of boyfriends.

On 1st December Norman came home from college and one of my good friends said she saw him looking 'cocky', riding a bike and showing off with just two fingers on the handlebars.

On 3rd December he rang me and my diary entry reads: *He has changed; he's all stuck up.*

On the 7th December I went to the Town Hall dance and Richard went too. Norman took a pretty, slim girl called Margaret Smith to the dance. My diary reads: *Norman came over and told me I knew nothing about horses. He has altered a lot.* This was like a slap in the face. Horses were my first love.

On the 14th I went to our school dance. It was held in the school assembly hall, still smelling of sweaty bodies because it was where we stripped down to our long-legged brown knickers and blouses and did gymnastics. On the wall were large wooden plaques recording our achievements. One read: *In 1946 Letty Broadhead was awarded the deportment prize.* I then had the honour of wearing a bright yellow sash around my dingy brown tunic.

That evening I was wearing a plain blue dress with red binding around my small waist from which my skirt flared out. My fashionable shoes were red wedgies. I remember these clothes although I did not write about them in my diary. I knew I looked good and was glad because Norman was there by himself.

I did not miss a dance and only had one bad moment when we played musical arms, where the men formed a line and held out one arm which the girls had to grasp when the music stopped. It was just my bad luck to find the music was turned off when I was opposite Norman and I had to hold his arm. He said, "Quite affectionate," and I said, "For a change." I remember these words although this also was not in my diary.

I danced most of the evening with Desmond Cole who was at Oxford University. He was tall, clever, interesting and funny. Norman was short and still a bit fat. My diary reads: *Norman looked a bit piqued.* School friends told me not to let Desmond go because one of the young teachers was after him. Desmond took me back to my house and on the way he criticized the architecture of some of the houses we passed. It was a pity he later went to live with the monks where he took an oath of silence.

The evening had ended with Briggs, Blyton, Hodge, and Stoodley, friends of Norman stealing some cakes from a cupboard in the school kitchen. These boys had all been prefects at the King's School and I knew them well. Our head teacher said there would be no more dances unless the culprits owned up and the cakes were returned. I believe they did return them.

Saturday, 28th December was the last dance of that year to be held at the Town Hall. Norman was there alone again. I went with three other boys in Cockerel's father's butchers van and had a super time. One of the dances was an excuse me waltz and, as I was dancing with one of my boyfriends, Norman tapped me on the shoulder and said, "Excuse me." Reluctantly I agreed to dance with him. My diary reads: *I told him off.* I may have said to him, "You are stuck up," or I might have said, "How dare you say I know nothing about horses?" There was only one short line about Norman as I had almost forgotten him, while there were five lines about my friends.

Norman is far left on the front row. He was 18 in 1946. Stoodley (who helped to steal the cakes) is middle front. Peter Boizot is in the second row far right.

Sadly I do not remember when Norman started to ring me again as my diary does not mention this. I only remember the first time we went out together was to my pony field and we were just good friends. Norman was very helpful and appreciative of my new mare and for about the first and last time in his life he was humble.

Soon the old magic of being in love came back but this time it was more realistic. I did not pretend my opinions were always the same as his and this time we recognized our failings while appreciating our good points. While Norman was at veterinary college and later, when I boarded at a college at Saffron Walden in Essex where I was training to be a teacher, Norman and I wrote to each other regularly.

My very old college had 'School for Mistresses' on a large notice on the top of its roof. Sadly this was not part of the curriculum.

Later Norman and I developed a passionate love which I learnt I was very good at. I also thought I had invented new aspects of love-making as I was so innocent, but I still kept Norman waiting for 'say cuff backwards'. I kept him waiting for five years. This was because my Mother threatened to turn me out if I became pregnant and also because a lovely girl in Norman's street had a baby out of wedlock and the neighbours would not talk to her or to her son. The baby's father was an American who was there to help us fight the war against the Germans.

Norman and me on a day trip to the coast, probably at Hunstanton.

Chapter Five

THE ENGAGEMENT RING

The engagement ring had quite a large diamond. My mother Hilda was the one who had first seen it in a pawn shop and knowing Norman was still a student thought it very good value. I think it cost about eight pounds. Norman's mother, who was also called Hilda, suggested it was lucky to put the ring on my finger near running water. So one dark night we walked to the Ferry Bridge about five miles away from Peterborough. Here Norman knelt down and proposed in the romantic times of the day. When bending down, to carefully find the ring he broke wind, just a little wind that was not noisy. He was terribly embarrassed.

Now, although we had known each other for about

six years, Norman had put me on a pedestal and he was very apologetic and sorry he had spoilt our special romantic moment. He was covered in confusion and bleated out how lovely I was and that he was a cad. I kept my laughter inside because I did not want to fall off the pedestal and also Norman was a serious chap with me and did not like to be laughed at. I was just glad the ring had not fallen into the swirling water.

By the River Nene before I became engaged. My mother told me to never lie down on the grass then I would not get pregnant. For a while I did as she said.

Two years before our engagement Norman had been out every night drinking with his mates in London. He had failed his exams at Camden Town Veterinary College and his grant had been stopped and he had to leave college. He needed to earn some money to pay for his fourth year there. At first, he worked at the Sugar Beet factory where he said the heat and moisture made his hair fall out. He then worked at the London Brick Company, doing night duty. Here he drove a train and once he fell asleep at the controls and hit another train that was on the same line. The cargo of messy spilt clay took a long while to clear up.

**The Ferry near Peterborough on the River Nene,
where Norman put the engagement ring on my finger.**

His mates were tough Italians who carried knives. Luckily Norman had a common look about him and he cycled to work, mimicking the Italians by wearing a small, dark beret on the side of his head. During a work break, while Norman was eating his bread and cheese, out would come his only friend, a small mouse, which appeared waggling its whiskers for food and Norman would waggle his own magnificent ginger moustache back. Norman eventually saved up enough money to return to college and if he passed the fourth year exams we were going to get married.

At the time I was teaching five-year-old children in one of the best state schools in Peterborough. I loved my work, especially teaching children to read. I tried to bring reading into every subject I taught, and years later I met one of my old pupils in Australia and he said he still remembered his first reading books which were about Old Lob and his farm.

In one corner of the room we had an old stove that burnt coke in winter. The back of the room was never heated, so during the afternoon when I told the children stories that I had learnt by heart, they would sit on the floor around this old coke fire, their rapt faces smiling up at me and they would join in the old familiar stories like *The Old Woman in the Vinegar Bottle* and afterwards we would act them.

When Norman and I finally married, one little boy wanted a wedding photograph just of me, but did not want Norman to be in the picture. I was so happy in this little school, but I knew if Norman passed his exams I should be joining him in Streatley on Thames for his final veterinary year. I would need to find a new teaching position.

I knew marriage was important to me as I did not like having sex and then walking away. An all night cuddle afterwards just finished it off. I was losing weight and sleeping badly because of this and my confidence was very low.

Hilda, my mother was as usual a great help. She suggested I ask Mr Tait, the Education Officer, if I could give in my notice at Queen's Drive infant school at the last moment. Mr Tait had a grand office in the Town hall and I remember climbing the imposing steps and knocking timidly at the big, oak, door. I felt very small and thin as I sat opposite the chief Education Officer, who looked tall and important, but I need not have worried. Mr Tait knew all about Norman and his failed exam. He smiled at me, and promised I could keep my job in Peterborough until Norman's exam results came through.

There were very few vets in England in 1951.There was just the one surgery in Whittlesey near Peterborough where Mr Poles senior, who had attended The Royal Veterinary College Camden Town when it first opened, and his son Sam had their veterinary practice. They were among the best large animal vets in England and Norman was very lucky to work for them in his holidays. They were experts on the treatment of horses and cattle and one of the practical tips they gave Norman was how to make a special blood-curdling cry that got a cow back on its feet when it had given up and lain down to die.

Sam and Norman often visited their farms on horseback and Norman learnt to ride, in a fashion. A good seat was very important in the horsey world, where nobody worried about class distinctions providing you could sit and ride a horse well.

Riding my new show mare, Royal Dancer. She poked out her nose too much and carried her tail badly but had a good confirmation.

I had been riding for years. Mother had bought my first pony, Bess, a milk cart pony, thirteen hands, for ten pounds when I was thirteen. I worked hard teaching myself riding from books Mother had bought for me.

When the pubs turned out at night, Sam and Norman used to visit small animals needing treatment. They drove a small, untidy van full of their own drugs, lotions and powders they had to mix up themselves. The two men wore caps on the side of their heads and had matching ginger moustaches and cheeky grins.

The stocky couple once visited our terrier, Judy. Sam knocked loudly and called out; "Are you there missus?" and my mother had to open the door in her night gown. Sam strode into the house wearing filthy Wellingtons and saying, "It's only good clean shit missus." My mother, like all the ladies, enjoyed being shocked by Sam.

What really embarrassed Norman was Sam's remark to the lady of the house, saying, "This is my new apprentice and you should see his huge dick. It is enormous." Sam was like a breath of fresh air in contrast to the ladies who were always trying to be genteel but were loving every moment of his naughty behaviour.

I was very proud that Norman was training to be a vet and anxious for him to qualify. He had told me the girls studying to be vets passed their exams by sitting on the examiner's knee. I never contradicted him in those days as men were supposed to know more than females.

I heard lots of interesting gossip if I just sat back and listened and did not look shocked.

I was glad most of Norman's hard drinking pals had left London and were in Streatley-on-Thames working for their finals. Norman was spending his fourth student year in lorry drivers' digs where he was given a huge breakfast which luckily mopped up some of his beer intake. Norman's older brother, Brian, had just qualified as a doctor at the famous St George's Hospital in London where he had married Barbara, a nurse. Brian knew I was not a well person and he told Norman to get his head down and do some work and then marry Letty and make her better.

Chapter Six

AT LAST NORMAN RANG

At last Norman rang from London to say he had passed his fourth year exams and we could be married. When his parents went on holiday we would put the bans up in the church. His father had forbidden him to marry before he had qualified as a vet, but once the bans had been put up three times his parents would be unable to stop the wedding. Norman said he had to ask Reg, my father, if he could marry me. This would be difficult because Reg thought Norman bossed me about. He often said, "He will have you in a mouse hole." If we received Reg's permission we would have just over four weeks to organise the wedding. There would not be time for us to fit in a honeymoon as I hoped to be teaching again in five weeks.

First I had to give in my notice at Queen's Drive School and find a new teaching post near the small towns of Streatley and Goring on Thames, where Norman was studying for his final veterinary year. After this, a wedding dress had to be bought and bridesmaid dresses made. Norman was going to hire an evening suit from Moss Bros. The invitations had to be printed and the Town Hall booked for our wedding. We would also have to find somewhere to live in Streatley.

My mum, dad and me. My mother always found clothes appropriate for the occasion.

Luckily my Mother enjoyed a challenge and I knew she would somehow make it all happen. My father was very good at making money and he was also very generous.

That night after Norman's phone call I lay awake, thinking about being married to one man for the rest of my life. We both loved animals and nature and Norman was a very good son to his mother. He was practical and a good, plain cook. He was not a snazzy dresser but made up for it with his charm and wonderful sense of humour - if he liked you! He never bored me and his life always seemed exciting.

Norman had a wonderful ear for music and complained bitterly if someone sang out of tune. He played the old pianos in the London pubs by ear, his left hand swinging backwards and forwards in the A flat key, which gave it more flourish. He played the favourite old songs with everyone joining in. The customers showed their appreciation by lining up the top of the piano with half pints of draught beer.

Norman and his water polo team were unbeaten.

Norman was a man of many talents and hobbies. At the King's Grammar School, Peterborough, he had won the much coveted prize for the best all rounder at sports and studies. He had excelled at most sports and he was captain of the water polo team which was unbeaten. He was coached by his father, Jimmy, who had been gassed in the First World War but later managed to be the reserve in the English Olympic water polo team.

Norman had also passed his higher exams studying the sciences, although he had to teach himself Chemistry because the science teacher was still in the armed forces. However, he was lazy at subjects he disliked and never did pass his French exams. When he decided to become a vet he started to work hard. Before this, his reports had been so bad that he had torn them up before his parents could see them. Luckily I did not like men who were too good.

Norman was a King Scout, school prefect and head of his house. I remember prefects had a yellow band circling their school caps. Norman's cap looked very peculiar stuck on top of his large crop of hair and big head.

Norman did not like his picture taken but this shows the yellow band.

Norman was also very good at woodwork and, aided by their pretty craft teacher whom they worshipped, he and Tony Bass made a large canoe.

Norman (about 16 years) is in front.

During the war we had to be careful the Germans did not drop bombs on us as they always flew over Peterborough on their way to London. We were forbidden to have any lights showing. Norman was very inventive and worked out how we could open his parents' back door at the same time as the light went off. He had studied electricity, so he fixed a wire to the inside of his parents' back door and then a loop of it was fixed to the overhead light so that when you opened the kitchen door the wire was tightened and the lights went out. I thought it was very lethal especially as tall people had to dodge the low hanging loop. Norman also bought a crystal set and made a wireless.

To make our marriage work I would need to share Norman's many interests and try and join in all his activities and listen to his plans. Norman was glad I was a good drinking partner and he was proud of my ability to down a half pint of draught beer quicker than some men. I could also hold my liquor well and was able to keep up with his hard drinking mates, many of whom were ex-servicemen. However, I was not a good cook and I was shy and lived in my own little world though I knew right inside me that I was strong.

I drank the best draught beer.

I also had a temper when I was roused. One evening

after a game of tennis, I was alone and leaving our park by a side entrance when a man sitting on a bike exposed himself to me. I hit him over the head with my racquet. The chain came off his bike and I chased him out of the park calling out for him to do himself up and not to show himself off again. Since I had been having sex with Norman, I considered myself a woman of the world.

A few days after Norman's telephone call he returned from London and he was ready to ask my father Reg for my hand in marriage. We waited until Reg was back from playing dominos and socialising at the pub and was in the dining room finishing off the evening with his nightly cup of rum. Reg was not an alcoholic but he liked his drink and most nights he was 'in his cups' which meant he was very happy and sometimes giggled a lot, so we used to leave him to drink in peace. However, there was no time to wait so Norman looking very determined set off for the dining room while Mum and I waited in the kitchen and tried hard to listen to what was going on.

Reg liked to relax by removing his collar and letting his braces dangle and there would have been mischief in his eyes as he saw Norman approach. His first words, we heard later, were, "You either need to borrow money or you want me daughter." When Norman said he wanted to marry me he replied, "Can you balance a cup of rum on your nose Norman? This is how it is done." It was easy for Reg to do this as he had a very big nose and also a sense of fun, both of which he had inherited from his illegitimate French ancestors on his mother's side. Then Norman again asked, "Can I marry your daughter?"

Reg, whose father was a Yorkshire man and who prided himself on his Yorkshire accent, said after a pause, "Gimme more time. I'll think on't."

And Norman walked away and said to me, "I shall marry you anyway."

My sister Jane's wedding photo, taken later as she is ten years younger than I am, shows the mischief in my father's expression. He is on the right.

The next morning just before 6.00am when most Brits were still sleeping until 8.00am, Norman's phone rang and, on answering it, he heard his future father-in-law say, "I'VE THOUGHT ON'T AND YOU CAN 'AVE HER!"

Chapter Seven

WE CONTACTED THE VICAR

Norman and I contacted the vicar of All Saint's Church, Peterborough, and our wedding was arranged to take place in just over three weeks. The vicar was very broad minded and said, "It does not matter if you are already joined together; marriage is a promise to stay together for life."

I thought back to when Norman and I first had sex. Before I let this happen I had asked him to accompany me to church to complete our union with God. Norman would have agreed to anything after waiting five years for me. While in the church I felt very uplifted but I expect Norman was only thinking of one thing. Now we had come to church again to read the marriage ceremony. I decided not to say *obey* although this was very unusual in 1952. I was thinking of my father Reg's remark. "He will have you in a mouse hole." I liked a man with a strong character but I also had my own opinions.

In those days it was usual for a man to collect you from your house, even if it meant walking several miles. He often bought you flowers. He walked on the outside of the pavement so that in bad weather he would be the one splashed by passing traffic. He stood up when a lady came into the room and he carried out the introductions. He opened doors for the ladies and let them go through first. He lent his big white handkerchief and offered his coat if they were cold. He would also expect me to like his friends but I knew he would not always be friendly to mine especially if they were a little bit boring. He did like animals and some children.

Norman nursing a kitten.

A happy Norman.

My mother Hilda enjoyed planning all the wedding arrangements. She was the boss and my father Reg liked to please her. She told Reg to find a very good second hand caravan that Norman and I could live in and a little second hand car that I would use for work. Norman left all the organization to mother because he could not interfere too much as he had no money and I did the same because I knew she was very good at making her plans come true.

Mother and I found there was a vacancy for a teaching post in Wallingford which was fairly near Norman's college and an interview was arranged.

Reg did provide a car for my interview in Wallingford. He found a very nice second hand caravan that he lent us and a year later sold it at a profit. He also bought me a little old Austin 7 tourer that I loved dearly.

Wallingford Church School was a Victorian building with high windows that the children could not see out of. There was an enormous tall wall around the school and beyond this was the village green or the Kine Croft as it was called. I was interviewed by the headmistress and the vicar who wore a long cloak and looked very intense. The headmistress was fairly young and modern and said I was not to teach the children reading until they were ready for it. This was my favourite very important subject and I would have declined the teaching post except Norman and I needed the money. I was accepted for the job and asked to start in three weeks time, two days after our wedding.

Later, Mother and I looked for a caravan site and we found a lovely one overlooking the river Thames at Burberry Road, Streatley near Norman's college. He would be able to cycle to college, while I drove to work. This site had spacious grounds and lots of apples trees and there was only one other caravan tucked around the corner from our site. Mother made sure she approved of the owners of the property. They were Mr and Mrs Beltcher who had retired there to grow vegetables and apples. I think they were asking seven shillings and sixpence a week for our rent.

Mrs Beltcher. She and her husband owned the market garden.

Me, wearing a Horrocks sun dress. Mr and Mrs Beltcher's bungalow is on the right.

My grandmother, Ethel, looked after the house while Mum and I went to Harrods in London for my wedding dress. We chose a classical lace dress with long sleeves and a train. Little did I know that about sixty years later, Princess Kate would wear an identical lace dress but with a longer train, when she married Prince William of England. My mother was a bright, clever lady with wonderful taste and she had helped me choose a wedding dress that was fit for a princess.

The men wore black pin-striped morning suits with top hats all hired from Moss Bros. Norman's father really fancied himself in a morning suit and he later ordered a new one that was made to measure. I expect he wore it when he went to the Masons Society. Norman was only about five foot seven and, with his hefty build and large ginger curled moustache and top hat, he posed for a photograph looking like the ringmaster at a circus. However, without the hat and wearing a happy smile he looked very handsome.

Me with my father, Reg, who gave me away.

The church was full. There seemed to be half of Peterborough there including some of my ex-pupils and their mums. When the ceremony started my father began to sob loudly and this went on throughout the service. It was a very hot day and while Norman and I were kneeling to be blessed, Norman, being a gentleman, passed me his new pure white handkerchief so that I could mop my brow. The congregation thought we were crying too just like my father Reg, whose sobs rang out louder than ever. He was a very emotional man and the music and the pretty wedding that mother had arranged for his daughter who he always considered delicate, made him happy and yet worried that Norman would have me in a mouse hole.

Chapter Eight

THE ONE NIGHT HONEYMOON

Norman and me with my sister Jane, my brother Mat and cousin Lesley.

After a very formal wedding reception at the Town Hall, Peterborough, Norman and I set off to spend the night at an ancient inn. While still at the Town Hall I changed from my wedding dress, that was the same as Princess Kate's, and put on a white grosgrain dress with a navy sash and a small navy hat with a white flower; just the sort of attire to wear in a shabby Austin 7 with the roof down.

Meanwhile our friends trimmed up our little car with lots of confetti and coloured paper, and old shoes and tins were tied to the back of it. Norman, with his large ginger, curly, moustache shining brightly in the sunshine, drove my little Austin 7 tourer.

The Neals: Brian, Father Jimmy and Norman who looked like a circus Ringmaster.

Spending one's wedding night in an ancient country

Inn was not a good idea in 1952. The staff followed us about with big grins, because in those days quite a lot of new brides were still virgins. Norman had a really bad hangover from his bachelor party which was always held the night before the wedding and where it was the custom for friends to spice the new groom's drinks. It must have been quite an ordeal for some of the virgins who had to cope with sex for the first time, sharing it with a clumsy hung over new husband.

After a good night's sleep we left our hotel early the next morning and drove to our new address 'The Westland' Burberry Rd, Streatley, Reading and I was delighted to see our caravan had been placed in a little circle of trees and positioned so that we could look out over the River Thames. There was only one other caravan and that was tucked around a corner as was the house of Mr and Mrs Belcher who owned the property. Norman carried me over the threshold of our new home. This was not easy as rickety caravan steps led up to the small door of the tiny separate kitchen and although I was tiny Norman was about fourteen stone.

There was plenty of room in our caravan because the bed pulled down from the wall and could be pushed back in the morning when the bed legs formed a little shelf. On this we kept our rent money in a little silver pot I had won at a gymkhana, and at night we tucked the pot containing our week's rent of seven and sixpence under the bed. We had no electricity, and used a little Tilly Lamp that had to be carefully pumped up or it burst into flames. We also had a small wood fire, that was cosy, but too near the bed for safety.

I was glad Norman was a practical, inventive man and could look after me. That was one of the reasons he appealed to me. We felt so happy in this warm little room, and outside there was the river and lots of trees and greenery and birds and even wild pheasants.

It was fun, and a challenge, to start a new life in different surroundings, meeting Norman's student's friends most of whom were older ex-service men, some of whom had been imprisoned during the war. When they first saw us sitting in our shabby Austin 7 tourer, they surrounded our old car and then these strong men, many of whom were rugger players picked up our car, with us in it and let it drop with a bang. All that happened was that our sturdy little car blinked its lights. Only a few of these men were married and I was the only wife with a career and earning money. Lots of the students had fathers who were prosperous vets, while Norman had a small grant and few possessions.

Norman in the little Austin 7 my father gave me.

Me, mending Norman's trousers while on our honeymoon.

I was horrified to find that, apart from his suit, he had only one pair of good trousers and a tattered pair that he asked me to mend on the only free day of my honeymoon. I was hopeless at sewing but for some reason very good at darning as it reminded me of weaving. Norman was excellent at sewing but once we were married I was supposed to take on all the wifely duties as well as my teaching in Wallingford.

Luckily he wanted me to join in his activities and that afternoon we hired a small dingy and I learnt to row a boat and Norman took a photo with a caption underneath saying

Our first row.

That evening we walked to the Bull Hotel which was an old coaching inn and where a pint of homemade scrumpy cider at eight pennies a pint made you feel wonderful. A bag of crisps was one penny and you could have a bath at the hotel for three pennies; soap, clean flannels and towels were included in the price. We turned on two bars of an electric fire and played darts. A night out for a shilling.

The old Bull Hotel had not been modernised and it was where Three Men in a Boat stayed to get their washing done before they sailed on to Wallingford where I was to teach school in the morning.

Chapter Nine

WALLINGFORD

Of a morning, it was lovely to wake up in our own little bed, but I had to hurry and make sandwiches for Norman's lunch at college, while I was having cheap, school, lunches in Wallingford. I had to leave early as the school was some distance away.

The caravan we lived in (note Norman's braces).

Norman did the man's thing like starting my little car by inserting a starting handle into a hole at the front of the car. It usually only took one swing to get the car going. I had the roof down and wore a fashionable headscarf and sang and whistled a tune as I happily drove my little Austin 7 along the quiet, unspoilt, countryside.

When it rained and the torn roof was put up, a little rain came through the passenger's side so when I was with Norman I put an umbrella up! I only drove at about fifty miles an hour and always enjoyed my Austin 7 because it handled like a small, nippy pony. When you wanted to turn right a little orange indicator shot out and if this was not working you shoved out your arm, or if you were turning left you turned your hand around anti-clockwise. When you changed gear you double declutched and you could really feel you were helping this little car along and knew when it was happy.

If I stopped at one of the small garages the men were always helpful at putting in my petrol, lifting the car bonnet to insert a little black stick into the oil gauge to see there was sufficient oil and topping up my water, as old cars needed water and oil frequently.

As I approached Wallingford, I passed the Kine Croft, or village green, on the left and then in front of me was my school - a sombre Victorian building looking like a prison.

In the Staff Room was the young vicar with a flowing cassock and an equally young headmistress who fancied him. She wanted modern methods of teaching which meant my five year olds had free expression most of the day and chose their own activities. This entailed playing with water or sand, creating models, and painting on large pieces of newspaper. I mixed together flour and salt and water to make material for the children to model. There was also imaginative play.

My Austin 7.

The children from Wallingford school.

Classes were big in 1952 and teaching was difficult with so many noisy activities. The quieter occupations using pencils, crayons, books, puzzles and dolls were not very popular.

Once I sent some children outside to do their

woodwork and they piled some boxes on top of each other and climbed up and, although the school gate was open, escaped over the wall. The older teachers disapproved of all these activities. One little boy, Freddy, who lived in a children's home cried loudly the whole morning. Luckily an older girl had been sent to help me on the first day.

There was one delightful little boy in my class called Johnny with an especially broad Berkshire accent. When I was cross with my class he would call out, "I didn't do it miss. It weren't me. I didn't do it." Nobody could make this long drawn out 'I' sound better than Johnny did.

Once, when I caught the bus to work, Norman met me outside of school in my little car. He was early, and while I was still inside the school, my class came outside and gazed with horror at Norman sitting in my car. He told me they surrounded my little Austin 7, but keeping their distance as Norman was a little frightening with his big ginger moustache. They stood there in silence with their eyes all boring into Norman so that he wondered what they would do next. He began to feel a little anxious. Then one brave little boy took a step forward and said very slowly and bravely, "Wot you a doing of in my Mistresses car?" I am sure that little boy was my special chum Johnny.

On the way home from school I called into the village

shop in Streatley. Food in England was still rationed, although this was 6 years after the war, and we all had ration books so that we could collect our few ounces of butter, bacon, cheese and meat a week. This small shop displayed no food in the window and there was little choice inside. The shop keeper was a crusty old soul who grabbed our ration books for keeps and weighed out our meagre rations, making sure we did not get a bit extra. I wondered how I was to feed a hefty young chap like Norman.

At first I dressed up with a hat and gloves, but later my dear mother, Hilda, sent me a duffle coat with a hood which had just been invented as the ultimate in leisure wear. Before this middle-class people had just one outfit for best until it became shabby and then they used this as everyday wear.

Me on my first shopping trip.

Once, I came home by bus. It was dark, and there was Norman, looking very dishevelled and apologetic, waiting for me. He said he was very, very, sorry he had taken all the rent money out of our special pot and spent it at the pub and he had twice fallen off his bicycle into a ditch. He promised never to do it again. I thought it very funny and was just glad he was alright and that my car had not been taken and damaged.

We lived on my wages of just a few pounds and saved Norman's small grant for emergencies and also for buying furniture for a house which would be provided for us when we worked for an established vet. I rarely nagged Norman about small things but when I was really angry my eyes would flash and I would sometimes throw things at him and he became very clever at dodging. Wives were expected to do everything for their husbands in 1952, and although Norman had put me on a pedestal he expected me to come off it and do most of the cooking, shopping and cleaning while he was revising for his final vet exams.

Chapter Ten

STREATLEY AND GORING PUBS

Goring on Thames village church.

Norman and I visited different old pubs on a Saturday night. These were cosy and unspoilt with ancient wooden beams above, and a warm fire burning in a vast old grate, with a collection of brass fire arms to poke and make up the fire. The floor consisted of spit and sawdust and the walls, discoloured by smoke, held shining horse brasses on their old leather straps. A group of locals would be sitting in their own special chairs playing dominoes, and smoking their old fashioned briar pipes. Behind a polished wooden bar 'mine host' was ready to welcome us.

"Miller of Mansfield Hotel" Goring

Here the students would gather and, later, we would sing dirty rugger songs which I found very daring as some of the words I had not used before. Most of these songs ended with an unhappy female either a pregnant one or a dead one. The men were very sexist and sang about these unfortunate females with gusto. I joined in some of them especially if they were about prostitutes who, back then, I used to think very wicked.

The bridge we had to cross to Goring as the pub there stayed open half an hour later.

The Streatley pub had to close at 10pm with the bar tender ringing a bell and shouting, "Last orders," and later, "Time gentle men please." We all giggled and swayed across the bridge a hundred yards down the road to the village of Goring where the pub had licensing hours until 10.30pm.

My new duffle coat to keep me warm while walking pub to pub 1952.

There was no food available in our pubs and none of us could afford to eat out so we filled up on cheap draught beer and crisps.

We were all so happy living in the pretty little villages of Goring and Streatley with the river close by and we loved the warm friendly antique pubs. I do not remember anyone shouting or quarrelling and only once was a student laid out on a table for a lark and I think beer was poured down his trousers but Norman told me not to look. During the Second World War, many of these men had been in the air force and some had their planes shot down over enemy lines and had been taken prisoner like Tom, Norman's best friend.

Walking home from the pubs helped to shake the beer down. Our caravan was warm and friendly with the fire still burning. We flung off our clothes, although Norman always hung up his only suit that was held up with braces. We pulled down the bed from the wall and I got in and waited. Sometimes I had a long wait. Norman had to find a condom and blow it up because at that time the occasional one had a hole in it. Norman said this was to keep up the population. First he had to rummage about to find a condom. Then he opened the wardrobe door and I would hear the antique brass plate fixed to the outside give a little clank, clank. While he was hiding behind this door I would hear lots of blowing up noises and the occasional swear word. Sometimes there was more rummaging until at last he emerged a little deflated and as the door closed behind him there would be a final chorus of clank, clank, 'success' at last from the brass plate.

Once we went to bed early and were almost asleep when an arm came through the open window beside me and then a voice we knew said, "Come to the pub." So we did.

In final veterinary year, a few horses and cows were kept for the students to practise on. On one occasion a veterinary instructor called out a very thin girl student and asked her to insert her hand and arm up a cow's bottom to find out what was wrong. It was a very cold day in the cow shed and the poor girl began to shiver and then her nose started to run. She rummaged around with one hand looking for a handkerchief while the teacher kept calling out, "What do you feel? Go in further then." The male students were as usual making fun of female students, but one of them did lend her his handkerchief. So, still with her arm inside the cow, she put the handkerchief to her nose and everybody waited to hear a loud blow but instead a little squeak came from her and the naughty students fell about laughing while the poor girl never did find the things she was looking for.

Norman told me many a story. Some were very naughty or were chauvinistic but I never criticized his tales because I knew if I did he would think twice before he told me anymore. I listened and sometimes laughed and I learnt some amazing things about young men because once Norman had a good audience he held nothing back. I stored up these little stories and pondered on them and many years later I began to realise how sexist most of the men were, but I also realised they had been brought up to be tough and 'to be a man' and later to be in control of their future household.

Norman's parents thought Christopher Robin was a sissy and he was not allowed to read his stories. Some gentle boys must have found this treatment difficult but

Norman had a pugnacious side to his character as well as a gentle caring side. Females were allowed the vote the year Norman was born in 1928. Before this a husband took over any money or property his wife had. It took a while for females to be equal partners.

The Swan at Streatley once owned by Danny La Rue. We never went there. It was posh and expensive.

Our local, The Bull Inn, Streatley. Scrumpy Cider 8 old pennies a pint.

THE BULL INN,
STREATLEY, BERKS.
J. GARDINER, Proprietor.

This House, being delightfully situated at the foot of the beautiful Hills, offers the best accommodation to parties visiting Streatley.

Splendid Ales on draught.
SUPERIOR WINES AND SPIRITS.
Well-aired Beds.

Chapter Eleven

THE AUSTIN 7 AGAIN

My life has been spent adapting myself to whatever situation I found myself in, and yet I have always been me. The first year of my marriage I was very shy unless I was in a pub where I had a few drinks. I did meet some of the student's wives who remarked how thin I was because it was fashionable to have a big bust like Jane Russel in 1952. They also did not approve of wives going out to work and thought my car very shabby.

**A veterinary college dance in London.
Norman and Letty are in the centre.**

Later, at a college dance in London, I met some older wives who were mostly married to ex-service men. Norman and I travelled to London in our little Austin 7 to a veterinary college dance where I enjoyed the company of the wives. They were amused when Norman and I won first prize for being the most inventive dancers, although Norman saved his energy and stood still most of the time while twirling me around. I ended up with my legs around Norman's neck and my hair sweeping the floor. In 1952 jiving was frowned upon as partners were always supposed to hold each others hands while the ladies left hand was on the man's shoulder and his right hand was around her waist. Even about fifteen years later a doctor's wife I played tennis with, saw me jiving and asked haughtily, "Where were you brought up?"

The little Austin 7 never let us down in our travels. One day I had a holiday and decided to drive on my own to historic Oxford. I stopped at the first antique shop I saw and bought a primitive hunting picture in a huge golden frame which my daughter, Sally, still has hanging in her bedroom. I also bought a bed-warming pan with a polished wooded handle. It would look good hanging on the wall in our future house. I used money from my four hundred pound building fund account which my mother and father had started when I was a baby. I never used this account for anything practical. This small account brought me endless pleasure.

The golden framed pictures and a bright polished warming pan looked happy sitting on the old leather back seat of my little car. They were tied on securely and nodded up and down to the beautiful Oxford buildings. Norman knew very little about antiques and when I returned said, "That's just what we need for our caravan." However, he never minded how I spent money from my account and he carried my purchases into a shed standing next to our caravan.

We inherited very large, magnificent early hand-coloured photographs of my Grandma Susannah and Grandfather William who were married in 1890. Each one was in a huge, ornate gold frame with brown velvet between the frame and the picture. We were told that Grandfather William fell off the wall if anyone in our family was going to die and, when we took a closer look, we saw his frame was very damaged at the top from when the picture had slidden down the wall. The photos were taken by Bamforth, an excellent portrait photographer from Holmfirth near Huddlesfield Yorkshire.

Photographs of my grandparents, Susannah and William Broadhead taken in 1890.

Photographs of my grandparents, Susannah and William Broadhead taken in 1890.

Norman and I knew Tony and Elizabeth Blyth, veterinary surgeons who were running their old family practice in Braintree. If Norman passed his finals he was going to work for them and we would be provided with a house. I should be sorry to leave our warm little caravan where Norman and I had been so happy but I looked forward to a proper bath instead of washing behind a huge plastic shower curtain once a week.

Most of all I would hate to sell my little Austin 7 which had become almost part of me. I loved the smell of the leather seats and the friendly dashboard.

Soon it was time for our first wedding anniversary and Norman booked a meal at the upper-class town of Frinton-on-the-Sea. I was dressed up and perfumed and wearing my best high heeled French shoes. Norman wore a clean shirt and tie but I could not persuade him to wear a jacket. When we arrive at the restaurant door, a very smartly dressed waiter held out his hand to stop us saying, "Gentlemen are only allowed in if they wear a jacket."

Our romantic evening flew away. We looked around for somewhere to eat but all we could find was a horrible restaurant with dirty windows and inside were greasy tables and a waitress with a grubby overall. A jute box was playing loudly. I remember there was a row of unattractive sauce bottles. The tomato sauce and Daddy's sauce had run down the side of the containers forming a horrible congealed mess.

Norman was happy with his usual fry-up but I could not eat anything and the tears fell plop, plop into the unappetising food.

This was the first of the minor tragedies in our life together, but I never let the tears come out again in public. Later on I learnt to manage Norman a bit better which made our life together more fun and certainly more adventurous.

Chapter Twelve

SIMBA

Norman did pass his final veterinary exams. We had to get ready to move to Braintree where Norman would start work. His father, Jimmy, was proud when son, Brian, had qualified as a doctor but Jimmy died before his naughty son Norman became a veterinary surgeon.

I mended the canvas hood of our Austin 7. We cleaned it up and, wearing my best sun suit, I sat in the driving seat and the car was soon sold. I was glad I approved of the man who bought it. My father took back the caravan and made a good profit, from the wedding present he had lent us. Mother looked after all our belongings as we were going to stay with our friends, the vets Elizabeth and Tony Blyth, until the house they were providing was ready for us to move in. Braintree was mainly a large animal practice, and I learnt to put Norman's shitty shirts to soak in a pail of cold water and not to mind Norman's smelly arm after he had treated a cow with milk fever. It was a sickly sweet smell and did not wear off for several days even after bathing.

Elizabeth and Tony were an unsophisticated, friendly couple and they had a couple of Great Danes - huge dogs that were allowed to sit up in the two antique chairs in the sitting room. I spent a lot of time with those dogs as Norman was busy working. Elizabeth was a vet but she did not help in the practice except to answer the phone.

We might have been living and working in Braintree for years but suddenly there was the Cold War with Russia and all young able men in England had to enlist. Norman had once tried to join the army in the Second World War but had been recognised by one of his father's friends as under age. The cold war was different. There was no fighting, just tension between the two countries and lots of preparations. Norman looked for an alternative solution. He could have joined The Horse Guards but for this he needed to have a good seat on a horse. He decided he would write and enlist in The Colonial Service and we could both have adventures.

A reply came back very quickly. Norman had been accepted to serve as a veterinary surgeon in Uganda,

Africa. Here the borders backed on to Kenya where the Kikuyu, a secretive tribe believing in black magic, were determined to get rid of all the colonials and settlers especially in formerly Kikuyu land, *The White Highlands*. They set up a sadistic secret society the Europeans called the *Mau Mau*. When extra police were sent out from England some of the Mau Mau started to escape over the border to Uganda where we were going to live.

I was very frightened but was determined to be with Norman where ever he was sent. My knowledge of Africa and especially of Uganda was very limited and my Grandma Ethel thought if I went I would be cooked in a large pot and eaten by cannibals.

Tony Blyth, the vet Norman was working with, had a friend who had lived in Africa and he came to give us good advice. He said, provided that we both had guns we would be all right. As soon as I heard this my knees started to shake and would not stop. Elizabeth helped me to my bed where I kept warm with the electric blanket. She brought me up a poached egg on toast and then I slept until morning. After that shock my knees never shook again, not even in Africa where I learnt how to fire a gun.

Norman and I flew to Uganda in an old Argonaut plane which had been used in the Second World War. I wore my best dress and high heel shoes as was the fashion for travel in 1953. Extra police flew with us ready to help with the Mau Mau uprising. The old aeroplane was taking us all the way but had to stop frequently to refuel while we sat on canvas chairs in draughty hangers. It took nearly three days to reach Entebbe in Uganda. There was no overnight accommodation. We enjoyed the food the air hostesses provided and we were not sick when our plane was thrown about in a very bad storm. Everybody else was ill; even the air hostesses.

From the plane we looked down on a vast, warm, empty country inhabited by wild animals and birds and we loved it. The African houses were mud huts with open doors and windows. We thought they must be dangerous accommodation little knowing we should soon be living in them for two weeks out of every month and eventually taking our new babies, Sally and Penny.

We arrived in Entebbe and were taken to the Imperial Hotel in Kampala where we were given a week to settle down and to buy a car which we would then drive to up country Soroti where we were to be based for two and a half years.

This is the end of my story but if I live long enough I would like to write of my beloved unspoilt Africa as it was then. It is a country I shall never forget and I want to remember it just as it was in 1953. I have never been back.

I started this chapter as a housewife in Braintree

England, a cosy little laid back ancient town. I have finished it at the Imperial Hotel with its starched white table cloths, gleaming cutlery elaborate menus and smart African waiters. This was the beginning of all the adventures Norman and I enjoyed throughout our lives together. I chose to marry the man I loved; an interesting talented man who could look after me. In our life together we had some stimulating heated discussions but we enjoyed adventures all our life and I was never bored.

On Safari in Uganda. The mud huts had open doors and windows and there was nothing in them. My high heeled shoes were very unsuitable.

Norman's nickname was "SIMBA' the lion because of his big ginger moustache.

Penny my daughter visited Uganda about six years ago. I was sad to hear this hotel had been boarded up and had a huge fence around it but I shall always remember how it looked in 1953.

The home that Simba built for me in Augusta, Australia.

Chapter Thirteen

LETTY'S TITBITS

Chapter 5

I improved Bess's feet by using a good blacksmith and I bought a crupper to put under her tail to hold the saddle back from her nonexistent shoulders. Bess bit, kicked and bucked and at first I was frightened of her but I had always wanted a pony so I did not give up trying to improve her. We eventually sold her at a profit as she was too small for me.

. . .

In my early childhood I had lived and attended school in the very bad slums of Peterborough. Later, my education had been excellent. I also trained myself to try to speak like the Queen, but I felt I was still inferior to some well bred people. The British were very class conscious in those days. Our town was much smaller in those days and most of the middle class people knew each other. The upper class people were still called 'the gentry' and in my pony club two of the boys were called 'Honourables'.

Chapter 6

The last interesting letter Norman sent me was all about his lorry drivers' digs and how big, fat Di, the daughter of the house who served up everyone's breakfast, was told she smelt and needed to take a bath. The trouble was she was so big, that once in the bath she could not get out. Her screams echoed throughout the building and the obliging lorry drivers put a bolt and tackle through the bathroom window to try to pull poor Di out. Another time whilst soaking in the bath (probably the same bath as Di used, as when I visited I only saw one) Norman was singing loudly in his fine baritone voice. He was heard by members of the D'Oyly Carte

Opera who lived opposite, and they came over and wanted him to join them, and train for their Gilbert and Sullivan Operas.

When playing sports I did not wear any make-up, but it was different when I went to the Saturday dance. I spent a lot of time on a Friday evening getting ready. I washed my hair and slept in curlers as we did not have hair dryers. In those days if a man asked you out they had to accept that you couldn't go because you were washing your hair. I also plucked my eyebrows on a Friday night and laid out a beautiful dress and French shoes and pretty underclothes including suspenders and new nylon stockings.

Towards the end of the war an American service man gave my Aunty Peggy, who was only seven years older than me, the first nylon stockings we had seen and we all crowded around her on the dance floor until she took one off and held it up to show us its transparency. My mother went shopping every afternoon and she often bought me all the luxuries she never had when she was young.

. . .

Norman appreciated me looking glamorous and wearing Chanel Number 5 perfume. He wore a suit with a tie and sometimes even borrowed his father's light weight dancing shoes. Now I knew him better, if he passed wind on the dance floor, he energetically twirled me around to keep people off the scent. I was glad we could laugh together and that I was allowed off my pedestal, but I knew I had to keep looking glamorous because Norman appreciated pretty women.

Chapter 7

Sometimes, when we were going on holiday, the car was packed and we were all sitting in it, Reg would appear and say, "Sorry I have sold this car but I will soon buy another one." However, occasionally, Reg would pay too much for a bad car and then there was trouble and we had to keep this scruffy looking vehicle for a long time and use it as our family car. Every time Reg approached the car he would give it a kick. Mother told me that they once went to a big posh wedding in a clapped-out mini, which was so awful they hid it behind a tree. The funny thing was that Reg had financed this wedding and also helped many of the guests in their shiny expensive cars because he was always lending money to people who he could trust and who needed help. They always paid him back, with interest.

When I told my Grandma Ethel, who lived with us, that we were getting married she said, "Do ye 'ave to? Well ye will be the first one in our family who didn't 'ave to." Ethel came from the ancient, superstitious Fen country, a place called Parson's Drove, a tiny hamlet with dykes on both sides; land that had been reclaimed from the marches. Her mother had been the unqualified nurse and midwife of the district, using herbs and unusual remedies, knowledge she passed on to her daughter, Ethel, who tried these cures out on me. When I had ear ache, she pushed the sharp inside bits of a heated onion into my ear. When I had whooping cough, she gave me a grey looking medicine that I found out later was boiled mouse juice.

These remedies had been used in the Fen Countries for generations. At night when my chilblains were sore, Ethel used rags to tie raw onions onto my toes. This seemed to cure them, but I imagined being married to Norman and wearing my new see through night dress with rosebuds embroidered around the hem and finishing this off with raw onions on my toes. I loved

Ethel, this kind wonderful person, deeply. Norman also loved my grandmother and on cold nights she poured him out a large whisky saying, "Git this down yer." She then filled up the whisky bottle with water.

I had an all white wedding. My Aunty Letty made the bridesmaids' dresses. To give them a crinoline effect, my Mother heated thin, long strips of wood until they could be bent into a circle and attached to the bottom of the dresses. Our bridesmaids were my sister Jane, twelve years, and my cousin Lesley, four years. My brother, six-year-old Matthew, was a pageboy wearing short white trousers and a long-sleeved top. My brother Bob, seventeen years, was an usher.

Chapter 8

I was happy at last to spend the whole night with someone I loved. Quick sex and walk away was not for me. I felt we were playing at Mummy and Daddy in this small but charming caravan. It reminded me of the little play house my father had once made for me, out of the back of an old van. This had shelves for my toy plates, and my dolls and I, had a little bed. I still felt very young and inexperienced and I think Norman probably felt the same except he had lived in London and some of his veterinary student friends had been sophisticated service men.

Chapter 9

My father, Reg, always brought back joints of cured bacon and eggs and butter from our farming relations, and we used to hang the bacon from the kitchen ceiling. Food rations in the war had given us: 4oz of bacon, meat to the value of 1/2d a week, 2oz of cheese, between 2oz and 4oz of cooking fat, 2-3 pints of milk weekly, 8oz sugar, 1 lb of preserves, every 2 months, 2 oz of tea, 1 egg per week sometimes dropping to 1 every 2 weeks, 1 pkt of dried egg every 4 weeks, 12 oz sweets every 4 weeks. Luckily sausages and offal were not rationed but, although difficult to obtain in the war, they were now easier to buy. Also, Wallingford had a market day once a week where I bought fruit and vegetables and a few treats.

I noticed nearly everyone in this county spoke with a strong Berkshire accent. To make the sound 'I', the lips were brought together and pushed forward as though blowing a musical instrument and then a *'yer'* finished it off at the back of the throat.

Norman learnt a little ditty which included a lot of these local *Is*. It included the word 'drawers' which is the ancient name for knickers. It goes like this:

Be I Berkshire, be I buggery, I come from old Sarum
   I got a gal with calico drawers, and I's know ow a tear em!

Chapter 11

My Grandfather William, a mill owner, died in March 1912 and Grandma Susannah moved to Folksworth near Peterborough where she kept cows and chickens and eventually married Mr Alf Hall who kept a Doss House for tramps and vagrants in the slums of Peterborough. He was also a general dealer. My father Reg liked the friendly characters in the slums and eventually started buying and selling cars and, when he married my mother, he bought a little house on the edge of the slums where I was born. Grandma Susannah loved her large pictures and made me promise to hang them on my wall when I had a house.

Norman was only twenty four and he must have found these unusual processions and my peculiar family very weird, but he loved my Grandmothers and he wanted to make me happy so he did not complain. However, he said when he qualified as a vet my little Austin 7 must be sold. I knew when Norman qualified he would be given a company car and vets' wives did not usually have their own cars or go out to work. I realized I would have to adapt to another world, walking to the shops, answering the phone to veterinary problems and leaving Norman's shirts which were caked with manure to soak in a bucket overnight. Vets had no protective covering in 1953 and few people had washing machines. I promised myself one day I would buy another old Austin 7 using my building fund account and perhaps then I would visit Oxford and Cambridge again.

The shower had a high shelf that housed a tin of hot water with a nozzle that we sprayed ourselves with. We had to boil up the kettle many times to fill up the tin and Norman showered after me and had to stand in my dirty water. The shower curtain was fixed to the ceiling inside our caravan. When my father Reg was buying this shower he had at first looked at it very dubiously until the salesperson had said, "What do you think it is - an elephant's French letter?"

Since I had been a little baby, cars had been my Wendy house to play in. When I was almost a year old Mother had bought me an early racing pedal car I could sit in. She had bid for this shabby racer at auction and probably only payed ten shillings for it because in 1931 England most countries were in the middle of a very bad recession. Mother had worked hard to restore this beautifully made little car. She later told me how she had cleaned and repaired it and then painted the car red. She had fixed a little old-fashioned hooter to the right of the car and taught me to press it. My father had put a small petrol can on the step. This was a little container for small tools. Finally my mother had placed me in the car with Toby, my small toy dog, sitting near me wearing a collar with 1931 written on it.

Afterword

Thank you for reading Letty's story.

Book Two : Sharing Uganda With Simba is
Coming Soon

Acknowledgments

Letty wishes to sincerely thank

Noreen Hacket who helped with the history for my writing,
Julie Matthews, Geoff McKinlay and Jan McKinlay who gave me great encouragement, Jan Brandreth and Marty Brandreth who encouraged me and who helped me with the editing and layout.

www.ingramcontent.com/pod-product-compliance
Lightning Source LLC
Chambersburg PA
CBHW060455080526
44584CB00015B/1444